PERIPHERAL VISION

A Book of Poetry Based on Scripture by
VIRGINIA NICKERSON

Wasteland Press

www.wastelandpress.net
Shelbyville, KY USA

Peripheral Vision:
A Book of Poetry Based on Scripture
by Virginia Nickerson

First Printing – December 2011
ISBN: 978-1-60047-657-0

Printed in the U.S.A.

0   1   2   3   4   5   6   7   8   9

FOREWORD

The ear that hears, the eye that sees, the Lord made them both.
                                        Proverbs 20:12 (NEB)

   Peripheral vision is what you see out of the corner of your eye when you're looking straight ahead.

   Though it can be measured with a field of vision test, an important diagnostic tool for your ophthalmologist, it is not intentional, it's never front and center, and it's definitely not what you are focused on. It's rather like a tangent in geometry, a line which touches but does not intersect a curve or curved surface and which then continues on its own direction. Sometimes what we see with our peripheral vision is distracting, but on occasion it can be important.

   Peripheral vision makes a good metaphor for what can happen as we read scripture. As a senior citizen who knows the who-what-why-when-where of most Bible stories backward and forward, I find that at times their plot and primary point become "old hat". But every so often those same verses, read from the corner of the eyes of my heart, will give me an *aha!* or *oh-oh!* insight that makes them new to me.

   I'd like to share some of these insights with you.

The Scripture quotations in these pages are from the following versions of the Bible:

   - *The Holy Bible, King James Version (KJV)*
   - *The Holy Bible, New International Version* (NIV)
   - *The Holy Bible, Revised Standard Version (RSV)*
   - *The Jerusalem Bible (JB)*
   - *The New English Bible (NEB)*

ABOUT THE AUTHOR

Virginia Nickerson grew up in the Midwest, attended the Bible Institute of Los Angeles (BIOLA), and studied nursing at St. Luke's Hospital School of Nursing in San Francisco and San Francisco State College, in that order. In 1951 she was appointed by the Women's American Baptist Foreign Mission Society for service in the Belgian Congo and after a first term, spent her first home leave studying midwifery in a program shared between the Maternity Center in New York City and Johns Hopkins Hospital in Baltimore. Virginia's years in Congo stretched from 1953 to her retirement in 1989; she counts as the most significant accomplishment of those years having a part in the formation of a three year nurses' training program for young men and women at Vanga, Congo *(Institut Technique Medical de Vanga.)* Today she lives at Pilgrim Place, a retirement community in Claremont, California.

AUTOBIOGRAPHY

The account of the wedding in Cana, at which Jesus turned water into wine, is a familiar one. You can read it for yourself in John 2:1-11. It is special to me because three times, in very different circumstances and times in my life, phrases from the story have had relevance for me beyond the simple telling of the tale.

I.

Whatsoever (Jesus) saith unto you, do it.
                                        John 2:5 (KJV)

The instructions were unlikely
but followed wholeheartedly,
   filling water pots
   up to the brim,
the liquid, decanted and carried
to the host of the feast
had been transformed--
   Behold! Good wine!

A young woman sought direction.
Whence this fascination with Africa?
   No family precedent,
   no particularly adventurous spirit--
just an idea that would not go away.
   God's still small voice?
   or monumental megalomania?

I obeyed what I thought I heard
and that obedience
opened the door to 36 years
as a missionary nurse in Congo.
It was a satisfying life--
   but I never stopped wondering

II.

Then (Jesus) told (the servants), "Now draw some out and take it to the master of the banquet." They did so, and the master of the banquet tasted the water that had been turned into wine. . .
John 2:8,9 (NIV)

Without trumpet or fanfare
water to wine
    marvelous, miraculous.

What adjectives to describe the life of a missionary?
    Satisfying? mostly.
    Dramatic? sometimes
but ever and always daily--
    same people, same programs
    same limited locale.
We lived in each other's pockets;
all was not well with our souls.

A visiting pastor from the states
spoke of an awakening in his church at home
reminding us of who and what we were meant to be
and somehow
profoundly and unexpectedly
it happened.
No tongues of fire
or mighty rushing wind
but there was transformation:
    irritation to empathy,
    pettiness to understanding:
our love was restored.

Wedding at Cana
or renewal in Congo:
    both were miracles.

III.

*The (Master of the banquet) called the bridegroom aside
and said, "Everyone brings out the choice wine first and then the
cheaper wine after the guests have had too much to drink; but you
have saved the best till now."*
John 2:9,10 (NIV)

Retirement: no more students,
   no more babies,
   no more missionary:
I was home to stay.

A long treasured verse about going out
   and coming in
and God's good care in both directions
was no longer needed:
   what now?

From this so familiar story
a new conviction
   subjective,
   out of context,
   and totally apropos:
the best saved for the last.

My heart cried out,
   Please, God,
   may this be so.
Amen and amen.

BARRIER

Therefore, if you are offering your gift at the altar and there remember that your brother has something against you, leave your gift there in front of the altar. First go and be reconciled to your brother; then come and offer your gift.

Matthew 5:23,24 (NIV)

I come to you, Lord,
and it surprises me
when you say
"Go first to your brother."
That faintest shadow between him and me
becomes an impenetrable wall
between me and you:
   the speck becomes a log,
   the inch a mile,
and I cannot reach you
though I try with pleadings and prayers.

Go first to my brother.
Your directive is specific,
and in that reaching out
I open the way into Your presence.

BEGINNINGS

In the beginning, God created the heavens and the earth. . .
And God saw everything that he had made, and, behold, it was
very good.

Genesis 1:1,31 (KJV)

At the beginning--
how many times have I stood there:
   a new year,
   a new project,
   a new resolution--
and how many times have I turned away,
and moved on to something else?

You who are both the beginning and the end
please, help me to stand firm to my purpose.
If indeed your Spirit calls me to it,
you can see me through to its completion.
Are you not both Alpha and Omega?

BOTTOM LINE

*(Jesus prayed) I have brought you glory by completing the
work you gave me to do.*
John 17:4 (NIV)

Will I ever be able to say that--
will I ever finish some of the many projects
that lie incomplete on my desk?

I start out so well, so often,
and then the work sits unfinished
as my level of enthusiasm ebbs away
and I turn to something new.

Remind me, Lord,
that it is not the beginning
but the completion of a task
that gives you glory.

BY CHANCE

Now by chance, a priest was going down that road... so
likewise a Levite. . . (and) a Samaritan.
Luke 10:31,32 (NEB)

I have some questions.

Was it totally by chance
for any of the three--
or even for the man beset by robbers?

Is not each circumstance
that comes into my life
touched by your good purpose for me,
either a demonstration of your love
or your call to action?

And I also wonder--
did the injured man ever recognize
that it was your love the Samaritan expressed
or the priest regret his failure
to be your man
in that situation?

CELEBRATION

And you will sing as on the night you celebrate a holy festival;
your hearts will rejoice as when people go up with flutes
to the mountain of the Lord, to the Rock of Israel.
                                    Isaiah 30:20 (KJB)

Dear God,
each time I read this verse
I am once again a pajama-clad child on Christmas Eve,
stocking carefully hung,
climbing the stairs on my way to bed,
a cloud of butterflies of expectation
dancing about my head.

I've never gone to the mountain of the Lord
to celebrate a holy festival
but I'm very sure that is how I would feel
if I did.

And I am equally sure that this is the attitude
with which you want me to live
even when life is daily;
ho-hum is never your adjective of choice.

COMPOST

True justice is the harvest reaped by peacemakers from seeds sown in a spirit of peace.

James 3:18 (NEB)

Jesus told a story about seeds
    and sowing
    and the size of the harvest
but it was mostly about
how the kind of soil the seed falls into
determines what it will produce.
He didn't say much about the sower.

This verse does
and it tells me
that the size of that harvest also depends on me.
The seed of your word
flung out in anger or self-righteous pride
holds not the same promise as the selfsame word
spoken in love and humility.

A meek and contrite heart makes good compost;
it enriches even the poorest of soils.

CONFIDENCE

As the time approached when he was to be taken up to heaven, (Jesus) set his face resolutely toward Jerusalem.
Luke 9:51 (NEB)

Lord Jesus,
when you told your disciples
that the man who puts his hand to the plow
and then looks back
is not fit for the Kingdom of God,
you were already on your way to Jerusalem.
Somehow you moved ahead
knowing full well
the end of your journey from its beginning.
Such courage you had, Lord;
how could you do it?

You know how often I quail before
the unknowns of tomorrow
even as I cling tenaciously
to yesterday's stale certainties.
As a result,
the furrow I dig with my spiritual plow
is shallow and wavering.

It wasn't courage, child--
it was confidence in my Father's good purpose;
is He not your father, too?

CONFLAGRATION

He will baptize you with the Holy Spirit and with fire. His shovel is ready in his hand and he will winnow his threshing-floor, the wheat he will gather into his granary, but he will burn the chaff on a fire that can never go out.
Matthew 3.11,12 (NEB)

O Lord, most Holy Spirit,
come as fire to me
to burn away the chaff of my life--
    the selfishness,
    the falseness,
    the judgments
that choke my soul
and contaminate my service for you.

May nothing remain but
ripened grains of wheat
destined for your granary
and for use as you determine--
    to make bread for the hungry
    or to sow as seed to bring forth
    thirty fold, sixty fold, an hundred fold
the harvest of your Spirit.

CONSTANCY

He who sent me is reliable. . . The one who sent me is with me; he has not left me alone.

John 8:25,29 (NIV)

So true,
and so wonderful.
Your faithfulness, Lord,
is what makes it possible for me to stay
in this difficult situation.

Circumstances change,
friends forget,
plans fail--
but you remain constant
and you are always with me.

When I find myself
between a rock and a hard place,
I am not alone.

COURAGE

"I am the Lord's servant," Mary answered. *"May it be to me as you have said."* Then the angel left her.

Luke 1:36 (NIV)

Where did it come from--
Mary's courage to say yes to the unknown?
Did the angel's explanation help?
or was it faith alone in the assurance
that she had found favor with God?

I'm aware that courage is essential not just for struggles
where enemies line up in battle positions;
I also need it for quiet moments
when my primary foe is fear of change
and I stand paralyzed, afraid to take the first step.

Dear God,
if it's your plan, I believe it will be good;
please--give me the courage to say *yes* to it.

CREATIVITY

Singers and dancers alike say, "All my springs are in You."
Psalm 87:7 (RSV)

God,
you alone
are the source of my creativity.
Whether I sing
    or dance
    or strum,
whether I work with words
    or paints
    or thread,
all I do to express my joy in your beauty
wells up from your Creator Spirit
flowing out of the river of living water
you have put within my innermost being.

For this, Lord, I thank you.

DEEP BREATHS

Come to me, all you who are weary and burdened, and I will give you rest.
Matthew 11:28 (NIV)

Mo ta pesa nge ntangu ya kupema.   (I will give you time to breathe!)
Matthew 11:28 (Kituba NT)

Dear God,
Yesterday was *one of those days* as I rushed
from pillar to post,
   from clinic to class,
   from dawn to dusk--
and on to the midnight hour at the maternity.

On a day like that
only your Kituba promise of *time to breathe*
keeps me going--
   your promise plus
   the wind of your energizing Holy Spirit
   and deep breaths on my part.

It's good to know
your promise has no expiration date!

DELAY

We want you not to become lazy, but to imitate those who through faith and patience are inheriting the promises.
                                        Hebrews 5:12 (NEB)

Lord, I do believe
that what you have promised
you will bring to pass,
but delay, like acid,
eats tiny pin holes
in the fabric of my faith
and my expectation oozes away
in diminutive droplets.

I ask you, Lord,
not just to help my unbelief
but to give me your patience
so I may wait for your promise
my expectation intact
and my faith flourishing.

DIMENSIONS

(I pray) that you, being rooted and grounded in love, may have the power to comprehend with all the saints what is the breadth and length and height and depth, and to know the love of Christ which surpasses knowledge, that you may be filled with all the fullness of God.

Ephesians 3:17,18 (RSV)

Dear God,
I marvel at the extent of your love for me.

Its length has carried me
    from teenager to senior citizen
    and ever *my times have been in your hands.*

Its breadth has stretched from California to Congo
    with the assurance
    Lo, I am with you always!

Its depth has delved
    into my innermost being
    when I have dared to pray, *Search me, and know my
        heart.*

Its height has soared
    to the mountaintop experiences
    where you have *borne me up on eagle's wings.*

Truly, Lord, your love for me
has ever surpassed my understanding.

DOORKEEPER

The words of the holy one, the true one, who has the key of
David, who opens and no one shall shut, who shuts and no one
opens.

Revelation 3:7 (NEB)

Dear God, I was so sure
this was your way for me.
but now the door is shut,
bricked over,
and I face a solid wall.
What now, Lord; what now?

I'm listening, Lord; I'm listening.
In this walled-in place
I wait your word
and your direction.
Your leading brought me here;
your leading must take me hence.

EMERGENCY

Suppose one of you has a friend who comes to him in the middle of the night and says, "My friend, lend me three loaves, for a friend has turned up at my house and I have nothing to offer him."

Luke 11:5,6 (NEB)

Lord,
make me such a one that friends
    or whoever in need
will feel free to come to me
    at whatever hour
    and with whatever need.
Help me to be truly loving,
    truly welcoming.

It's so easy to turn people away
with a closed face
    or a cold word.
Forgive me for putting my program,
    my priorities
    my privacy
between me and the people
You want me to serve.

EQUATION

*They were on the road, going up to Jerusalem, Jesus
leading the way; and the disciples were filled with awe; while
those who followed behind were afraid.*

Mark 10:32 (NEB)

Lord Jesus,
it's not *"pi times the radius squared"* but
it makes a great equation:
    Fear increases in inverse proportion to
    how close I stay to you
    or
    The greater the distance between us
    the higher my apprehensions and anxieties loom.

Why is it so easy to lag behind,
    side-tracked by circumstances or
    dawdling over daily duties?
I intend to walk close beside you,
and then here I am again,
    worrying about all manner of things
    and you are almost out of sight.

My friend,
you could run to catch up.
I'll wait for you while you do.

ESSENTIAL

A woman named Martha welcomed Jesus in her home. (Her) sister Mary sat down at the feet of the Lord and listened to his teaching. Martha was upset over all the work she had to do, so she came and said, "Lord, tell (my sister) to come and help me." The Lord answered her, "Martha, Martha! You are worried and troubled over so many things, but just one thing is needed. . . Mary has chosen the right thing, and it will not be taken away from her."

Luke 10:38,40 (GNB)

Dear God,
It's so easy to fuss and fret
about all sorts of things
and sometimes I grow cross and unloving
even as I do them in your name.

My mind knows
that it is not what I do
but what I become
if I stay close to you
that is the important thing.

Please, God,
keep reminding me--
I forget so quickly

EXCHANGE

Thou hast turned for me my mourning into dancing;
  thou has put off my sackcloth,
   and girded me with gladness;
to the end that my glory may sing praise to thee,
  and will not be silent.
O Lord my God, I will give thanks unto thee for ever.
                    Psalm 30:11,12 (KJ)

Dear God,

Dancing instead of mourning?
  a new robe to replace sackcloth?
  throw in a girdle of gladness?
No way is this exchange *even-stephen.*

These gifts are born solely of your grace,
  and you delight to give them
  as much as I delight to receive them.
How can I ever thank you?

I agree with the psalmist--
  it will take forever
  so I'll start now:
Thank you, Lord…

Very much.

EXPECTATIONS

When all the people saw (the man) walking and praising God, they recognized him as the same man who used to sit begging at the temple gate (and they) were astonished. Peter. . . said to them, "Men of Israel, why does this surprise you?"

Acts 3:9-12 (NIV)

Why indeed?
My mind knows you can do all things
but my heart expects so little.
I must confess your intervention leaves me
shaking my head in wonder.
Is not expectation
just another name for faith?

Please, Lord,
make my faith
grow to meet your promises
so that I am not taken by surprise
at the range of your doings.

FIRST THINGS FIRST

*On coming to the house, (the kings) saw the child with his
mother, Mary, and they bowed down and worshiped him. Then
they opened their treasures and presented him with gifts of gold
and of incense and of myrrh.*
Matthew 2:11 (NIV)

First things first:
Mary believed the angel
and praised God for his goodness.

First things first:
the shepherds left their flocks
and hurried to find that newborn child.

First things first:
the wise men traveled scorching starlit distances
and worshiped the child when they found him.

First things first:
that child, full grown
tells me to seek first God's kingdom.

First things first:
and I am the one who sets my priorities,
and I am the one who schedules my days.

First things first.

FOCUS

Mary. . .seated herself at the Lord's feet and stayed there, listening to his words. .. (Jesus said) 'The part that Mary has chosen is best, and it shall not be taken away from her.
Luke 11:39-42 (NEB)

I.
Mary sat.
No jumping to put away the broom,
no fidgeting over the bed still unmade,
her body and her mind at rest,
    Mary sat at Jesus' feet.

Mary stayed.
No eye on the clock,
no sense of time limits,
no hurry, no pressure
    Mary stayed.

Mary listened.
And because she had put aside the distractions
of household and hurry
she could hear.
    Mary heard beyond the words.

Jesus said Mary chose the best part.
Did Martha realize there was enough "best"
    for her, too?

FOCUS (II)

*Mary. . .seated herself at the Lord's feet and stayed there,
listening to his words. .. (Jesus said) 'The part that Mary has
chosen is best, and it shall not be taken away from her.*
Luke 11:39-42 (NEB)

It's paradoxical--
the single simple part that Mary chose
encompassed all that was important
while Martha's multiplicity of purpose
crowded out the one matter
that was truly essential.

Isn't there a promise
that if we seek his kingdom first,
God will give us all else beside?

FOR ALL SEASONS

And now, O Israel, what does the Lord your God ask of you
but to fear the Lord your God, to walk in all his ways, to love him,
and to serve (him) with all your heart and with all your soul. . .
Then I will send rain on your land in its season, both autumn and
spring rains, so that you may gather in your grain, new wine and
oil. . . And you will eat and be satisfied.
                              Deuteronomy 10:12, 11:14 (NIV)

Lord,
I remember the spring rains--
the time of your first calling
and my first response.

The paths where you have led these many years
have been good
but now it is summer
and my soul has become dry.
Only the promise of new refreshing
sustains me in this dusty place.
I wait the autumn rains
and the time of harvest:
        new wine and new joy,
          fresh oil and fresh anointing
for tomorrows yet undawned
and tasks still undreamed.

Truly, Lord, you are a God for all seasons.

FOR SURE

For I am certain of this: neither death nor life, no angel, no
prince, nothing that exists, nothing still to come, not any power, or
height or depth, nor any created thing, can ever come between us
and the love of God made visible in Christ Jesus our Lord.
Romans 8:38,39 (JB)

What-if? asks the child, making it one word,
counting off a child's garden of horrors:
      What-if I can't keep up?
      What-if I fail the test?
      What-if no one will sit by me?
What-if? What-if?

I have my own catalog of calamities
when I wake too soon in the dark of night:
      What-if it's malignant?
      What-if they waited too long?
      What-if I have to have chemo?
What-if? What-if?

The questions resonate like buzzing mosquitoes
Until God's quiet indwelling Spirit jogs my memory:
      For sure, my times are in God's hand;
      For sure, God is always with me;
      For sure, nothing can separate me from God's love.
For sure. FOR SURE!

GAME PLAYING

Then Judas, already turned traitor, said, "It isn't me, is it rabbi?" Jesus said, "Don't play games with me, Judas."
                    Matthew 26:26 (The Message)

Play games with Jesus--
if I'm honest
I have to admit that sometimes
I've done that.

I've sung about sweet hours of prayer
while my schedules and routines
crowded out daily quiet time

And I've tithed to the decimal point
while I failed to love my neighbor
or neglected responsibilities I didn't want.

There are even times when
my rendition of the gospel song
should have come to a dead stop at
    "Take my life and let it be!"

Judas isn't the only game player.

GOOD GIVING

All good giving, every perfect gift, comes from above, from the Father of the lights of heaven.

James 1:17 (NEB)

Not just the gifts you give me, Lord
    so generously,
    so freely,
but the ones you prompt me to give to others.

I cling so to things
and hoard them for myself,
stashed away on shelves
or hidden in boxes
    for tomorrow,
    just in case
and when I get them down again
    they are mildewed,
    rusted,
    tarnished
and I have neither the joy of my possession
    or the delight of having given.

Teach me to give, Lord, as you give--
gifts that are timely,
    needed,
    joyful,
knowing it is impossible
to outgive your generosity to me
and that failure to give
is to quench the prompting
of your Spirit.

HOSPITALITY

While they were on their way, Jesus came to a village
where a woman named Martha made him welcome in her home.
She had a sister named Mary, who seated herself at the Lord's feet
and stayed there listening to his words. . .

Luke 10:38-42 (NEB)

How beautiful the gift of true hospitality:
a gift without ulterior motive
measured by the size of the heart
not of the hearth;
it is learned from no handbook
practiced with no guile
and never listed in catalogs.

It is a gift that outshines Good Housekeeping
and the Martha in question is not Martha Stewart.

* * * * * *

Interesting that it was Martha's house,
not Martha's and Mary's together.
Was Martha house proud?
And was everything so perfect
it couldn't be comfortable?

Mary's gift of attention
was greater balm to Jesus' spirit
than the shine of smudgeless brasses
and a perfectly appointed table.
Teach me, Lord, what your gift of hospitality
really consists of.

IDENTITY

*I am the Lord, unchanging; and you, too, have not ceased
to be Sons of Jacob.*

Malachi 3:6 (NEB)

How good, Lord, to know
not just who You are
but who I am in your sight:
    your daughter,
    chosen, elect,
    eternally loved.

How often I fail
to live up to the faith I profess
and despair of myself,
    even to questioning
    my identity,
until you remind me
that in your constancy
I cannot cease to be other than your child.

(IM)PATIENCE

At sunset all who had friends suffering from one disease or
another brought them to (Jesus).

Luke 4:40 (NEB)

They had waited all day
because it was the Sabbath,
and they dared not come before the sun had set
    lest they incur the ire of the Pharisees.

They had yet to learn
that the Sabbath was made for man,
not man for the Sabbath--
    but they did not wait patiently.

IN DUE SEASON

And let us not be weary in well doing; for in due season we shall reap, if we faint not.

Galatians 6:9 (KJV)

Forgive me, Lord, when I do just that--
when I grow weary in well doing.
and am tempted to turn back.
I don't faint,
but just as bad or even worse,
I plod on in deadly, dutiful drudgery
while your way is meant to be
refreshment!
    and adventure!!
      and alleluia!!!

I know this in theory--
please, Lord, help me to live it.

JOY FOR TODAY

(Jesus said) "I speak these words so that (my disciples) may have my joy within them in full measure."

John 17:13 NEB

Lord Jesus,
you always give abundantly:
   fresh joy,
   new every morning,
   pressed down and running over.

Teach me to receive
the same way you give:
   my arms outstretched to embrace
   each new day,
   each new circumstance.

Are not these the packaging
in which your joy is delivered?

MEMORY LOSS

This is the covenant that I will make with them. . .says the Lord: I will put my laws on their hearts, and write them on their minds. Then he adds, I will remember their sins and their misdeeds no more.

Hebrews 10:16,17 (RSV)

Dear God,
I rejoice when you tell me
you no longer remember my many failures
but when I forget
a meeting I was supposed to attend,
it scares me.

Your *forgetting* is deliberate;
mine is never intentional
and I am left wondering--
is it the normal slowdown
that can come with advancing years
or is it a first indication of
oncoming Alzheimer's?

Which indeed?
Whichever, I'm sure
You will be there with me!

MINDSET

*(Jesus) sent messengers ahead...into a Samaritan village...
but the villagers would not have him because he was making for
Jerusalem. . . (so) they went on to another village.*
Luke 9:51-56 (NEB)

Lord, I've read of how
when Jews traveled between Galilee and Judea
they avoided Samaria,
going the long way round
twice fording the Jordan
because *"Jews have no dealings with the Samaritans."*

I'm impressed that you took
the straightest road,
the shortest time,
so your purpose might be the sooner accomplished.

And I marvel, too,
that the Samaritans animosity and rejection
neither slowed you down
nor turned you from your course
as you strode on to the next village
and the next
all the way to Jerusalem.

How often my angry reactions
dissipate the drive meant to carry me forward
and I end up spinning my wheels furiously,
digging ever deeper into a rut of resentment and rebellion
that writes *finis* to any progress.

MIRROR IMAGE

Now Martha was distracted by her many tasks, so she came to (Jesus) and said, 'Lord, do you not care that my sister has left me to get on with the work by myself? Tell her to come and lend a hand. But the Lord answered, 'Martha, Martha, you are fretting and fussing about so many things, but one thing is necessary. The part that Mary has chosen is best, and it shall not be taken away from her.'

Luke 10:40-42 NEB

I laugh when I read about Martha
for I know that I am reading about myself--
    disturbed,
    distracted,
     poor-me
and don't you care?

You do care, very much indeed
and that is why you didn't
accede to Martha's demands
and direct her sister
to run to her rescue.

Martha didn't need help with the housework;
she needed to get her priorities straight--
as do I.

MY CHOICE

*As they were marching out, (the soldiers) came upon a man
of Cyrene, Simon by name; this man they compelled to carry
(Jesus') cross.*

Matthew 27:32 (RSV)

Sometimes I think
it would be easier
if, like Simon,
You forced me to take up my cross
but then I know
that the real glory of any cross
lies in the glad acceptance of it
and only free choice
can make it truly bearable
and productive.

Nothing and no one
can make me bear its pain;
nothing and no one,
save myself alone,
can cheat me of the glory
and the blessing
You mean it to be in my life.

NO GUARANTEE

Then the word of the Lord came to (Elijah): Leave this
place and turn eastwards; and go into hiding in the ravine of
Kerith east of Jordan. You shall drink from the stream. . . (Elijah)
did as the Lord had told him. . . After a while the stream dried up.

I Kings 17:2-7 (NEB)

Dear God
I have a question.

It was your unmistakable direction
and Elijah's wholehearted response
that took him to that place;
how then could the brook of your provision
diminish to a silent trickle
and finally evaporate completely
under the scorching sky?
Surely at the crossroad of your promise
and his obedience
brooks should not dry up
or enterprises fail.

Am I wrong to think that
obedience should guarantee success
or that the place of total obedience
is always a place of total security?

What have I missed?

NO WAY!

> *But (the disciples) understood nothing of all this; they did not grasp what (Jesus) was talking about: its meaning was concealed from them.*
>
> Luke 18:34 (NEB)

Lord, the words could hardly be clearer--
was it truly they could understand?
Or was it that they refused to hear
with a flat, let's-have-no-discussion
"Not so, Lord"-- like Peter
the way I often say "No way, God,"
when You try to lead me
into new areas of doing or thinking.
"No way" maintains my comfortable status quo
but it makes me a spiritual stick-in-the-mud
with no growing edge
and very muddy boots.

Very true, my friend, and have you noticed
your resistance increases
the closer my new word brings you to the cross?

OCTOGENARIAN

(And Caleb said) Behold, the Lord has kept me alive these
forty five years. . . and now, lo, I am this day eighty-five years old
(and) I am still as strong to this day as I was in the day that Moses
sent me (and) my strength now is as my strength was then. . .
Joshua 14:10,11 (RSV)

Dear God--
I, too. am a fellow octogenarian
but I'm certainly not a Caleb.

No way am I as strong as I was in my thirties and forties
but even so
I find my eighty's good--
    with new friends
    new challenges.
    and ever new days, bright with sunlight.
What hasn't changed is You--
    your care
    our keeping
    and your mercies, new every morning

Frankly, it's my opinion
Caleb was exaggerating.

OVERCAST

*As the priests were leaving the temple, it was suddenly
filled with a cloud shining with the dazzling light of the Lord's
presence.*

                                        I Kings 8:10,11 (TEV)

Lord,
the clouds of my life don't dazzle--
they hang low on the horizon,
murky metaphors for
today's tensions and tomorrow's terrors.

They shut out
and they close in,
and I stand isolated,
yearning for sunlit fields
and the light of your presence.

I don't ask that you take the clouds away
but that you color them luminescent,
not leaden.
I want to see you in spite of them;
I want to recognize you in them.

PERSEVERANCE

Consider it pure joy, my brothers, whenever you face trials
of many kinds, because you know that the testing of your faith
develops perseverance (and) perseverance must finish its work so
that you may be mature and complete.

James 1:2,3 (NIV)

It sounds fancier with a British accent:
 per-SE-ver-ance
but it still means the same thing:
 hang in, and try again;
 hang in, and see it through;
 hang in, and go the second mile--
and sometimes even a third.

If that's the road to maturity
it sounds like a very rocky road indeed,
and I'm going to need help--
a lot of help.

Obviously, *hanging out* and *hanging in*
are two very different matters.

PHONY

(Judas) said this, not out of any care for the poor, but because he was a thief: he used to pilfer the money.

John 12:6 (NEB)

I don't steal, Lord,
but sometimes I act
    or speak
in such a way
that others will think
I am more spiritual
than I know myself to be.

I don't want to blow my missionary image,
so I set my smile
    and soften my voice,
and people call me dedicated
even as my blood pressure soars.

PIQUANCY

There are days when I feel like that, Lord--
perhaps not totally tasteless
but insipid,
bland,
and boring.

You who can restore the years the locusts have eaten--
can you not restore my savor?
I ask that you touch me again
so I may be salty
piquant
and aglow with your Spirit.

Mixed metaphors indeed
but you know what I mean.

POLLUTION

(Jesus said) *And if anyone will not receive you or listen to your words, shake off the dust from your feet as you leave that house or town.*

Matthew 10:14 (RSV)

Am I missing something, Lord?
These words sound so harsh
even petulant or childish
with echoes of *all-right-for-you*
and *nyah-nyah-nyah.*
What is it you are saying?

My child,
can you not see
that the dust of which I speak
is the residue of resentments
born of hurt feelings and rejection?
Carried with you
they will become pollutants and irritants
that dull your outlook
and blur your vision.
I want you to come fresh,
open,
receptive
to each new place and situation.

Only then will you have peace to give
to the house you enter.

PONDERING

*But Mary treasured up all these things and pondered them
in her heart.*   Luke 2:19 (NIV)

So much to remember--
    the fatigue of the journey
    the pain of the delivery
so much to consider--
    the angel's greeting, the shepherds' tale,
    the kings, the gifts, the star
and now so much to do--
    the home to be maintained
    the care of the child
where was there time to sit and meditate?

It had to be as she nursed her son,
    prepared food, carried water,
    spread new rushes on the floor--
the only quiet Mary knew was the quiet of her heart.

I didn't expect to find multi-tasking
in the Christmas story--
but it's there between the lines
and I ask myself--
will it work for me?

As unlit candles on my Advent wreathe
bear witness to my "too busy"
I wonder, Could I ponder and pray
while I wrap gifts, bake cookies
and address Christmas cards?

It's worth a try.

PRAYER REQUEST

Jesus said to him, 'What do you want me to do for you?'
'Master,' the blind man answered, 'I want my sight back.' Jesus
said to him, 'Go; your faith has cured you.' And at once he
recovered his sight and followed (Jesus) on the road.
                                    Mark 10:51,52 (NEB)

Dear God,
I can't help wondering
what if the blind man had asked for less--
    food to fill his hungry stomach
    coins to take home to his family
    a warm wrap to place about his shoulders--
or even a seeing-eye dog
(if such existed them.)
Any of these requests would have been more reasonable!

Could it be that I miss blessings
You would delight to give me
because I don't ask enough?
I don't want to settle
for something small or pinch-penny
when all your love
and all your resources
wait my request.

PRESUMPTION

Happy that servant who is found at his task when his master comes.

Luke 12:43 (NEB)

Lord, you know
that this verse has spoken to me
of how I must keep busy
about your work.
I must do this, then that,
and always there is more to do
and surely the King's business requires haste.

But this morning, Lord,
it says something new:
You want me to do
those specific tasks you ask of me,
and if I take on my brother's responsibility,
it is not only pointless.
it is presumptuous.

PRIORITY MATTER

Simon's mother-in-law was ill in bed with fever. They told (Jesus) about her at once. He came forward, took her by the hand, and helped her to her feet. The fever left her.
Mark 1:30 (NEB)

How often, God,
when I meet difficulties
do I bring them to you
only as a last resort--
after I've worried and fretted
and very possibly made the situation worse
with my *do something!*
(and *do it now!!)*
attitude.

Will I ever learn
solutions start with prayer?
and I should put matters into your hands
 from the *get-go?*
Not only would it save wear and tear on my nerves,
I would be practicing what you tell your children to do--
casting all my care on you.

PROMISES

But, Sir, Gideon replied, if the Lord is with us, why has all this happened to us? Where are all his wonders our fathers told us about?

Judges 6:13 (NIV)

Lord,
I'd never say that
because I'm a Christian
and we Christians have your promise
that *all things work together for good.*
Even so, I must admit
sometimes I think it
and even a specific promise is not enough.

My friend,
it is not the promise you must trust
but the One who promised.
Did I not say
I would be with you always?
Surely that includes today,
whatever its circumstances.
Trust me.

PROMISSORY NOTE

Faithful is he that calleth you, who also will do it.
I Thessalonians 5:24 (KJV)

I remember the day
I packed my freight to send to Congo.

I had several out-sized cardboard boxes,
    a vintage steamer trunk,
    and one metal drum.
Into these I put
    clothing and linens (the steamer trunk)
    plastic dishes and cooking pots (the drum)
    and oddly shaped miscellany,
all snuggly ensconced in a year's supply of toilet paper.

Then, last of all,
into any remaining virtual crack or crevice
I tucked this promise
to sustain me in my new venture.

The uniforms wore out in months;
the pressure cooker blew up my first term;
a decade later I gave the plastic dishes, still intact,
to Tata Fanga, *houseboy extraordinaire.*
Only the much claimed promise survived
all my decades in Congo;
and was still as good as new.
when I came home to retire.

To this day,
it continues to serve me well.

PROXIMITY

Stay close to the king, wherever he goes.

II Kings 11:8b, NIV

God,
I know these words aren't talking
about relationship,
but that is what they say to me.

Stay close to your king--
is not this what Jesus meant
when he told us
to seek first the kingdom of God?

PURSUIT OF HAPPINESS

The ransomed of the Lord will return.
  They will enter Zion with singing;
    Everlasting joy will crown their heads.
Gladness and joy will overtake them,
  And sorrow and sighing will flee away.

Isaiah 51:11b (NIV)

Dear God,

  This is not the American way--
we're brought up on the pursuit of happiness,
and we spend much of our time
    trying to run it down.

  Your way is different.
When our eyes are fixed on you
and our efforts expended in serving others,
    happiness can overtake us.

  When we run after it,
it slips from our grasp.
This way, the grasp is yours
    as well as the gift.

QUESTIONS

You are right, Lord--
There is much I do not understand
And I frequently ask
Why this?
or *Why now?*
and sometimes even *Why me?*
But even as I question
I know what You will answer:
This, to give you glory,
Now, because this is your timing
and *Me,* so I can grow in your love.

I apologize for my questions
and, please, Lord,
forgive me when I ask them again.

RAW MATERIAL

Their weakness was turned to strength.

Hebrews 11:34 (NEB)

I marvel, Lord, at these heroes of the faith:
   undaunted in difficulty,
   ever obedient in their belief;
surely they are made of other stuff than I.

But then I read
   that weakness was the raw material
   of which these spiritual giants
were conceived.

Weakness--
   plus the presence and the power
   of your Holy Spirit.
That means there's hope for me, too.

Am I right?

RELATIONSHIP

Then King David went into the Tent of the Lord's presence,
sat down and prayed, "I am not worthy of what you have already
done for me, Sovereign Lord. . . yet now you are doing even more.
What more can I say to you! You know me, your servant. . . How
great you are!

II Samuel 7:18-20 (GNB)

You also know me, Lord,
inside and out:
    the tensions,
    the dissemblances,
    the motivations.
You know me better than I know myself.

This would be a scary thought
except that I know you, too--
    your good purpose for me
    your daily care
    your constant provision.
and knowing you, I am not afraid.

But I do marvel
that knowing me so well
you love me still.
How can I be other than your servant?

RENDEZVOUS

But go, tell his disciples and Peter, 'He is going ahead of you into Galilee. There you will see him, just as he told you.

Mark 16:7 (NIV)

He is going ahead of you.
Underline the words
and rejoice, rejoice greatly.

A new job? A new experience?
Something you face with joyful anticipation?
Or a return to a place or situation that was painful--
    into the doctor's office,
    into the surgery,
    into the very valley of the shadow of death?
Whichever it is,
He goes ahead of you
    to prepare
even as he walks beside you
    to sustain and encourage.

Truly, any situation can be Galilee,
and any geographic spot the place of meeting with Jesus,
and there you will see him, just as he promised.

RESOLUTION

Though the fig tree do not blossom, nor the fruit be on the vines,
*   the produce of the olive fail and the fields yield no food,*
the flock be cut off from the fold and there be no herd in the stalls--
*   yet I will rejoice in the Lord,*
I will joy in the God of my salvation!
                                    Habakkuk 3:17,18 (KJB)

As a teenager
I sang with my friends
*   I have decided to follow Jesus. . .*
*   no turning back,*
*   no turning back.*
That decision took me to Congo
and life was good.

Today in retirement I've added
a three letter codicil to that initial promise--
*   no matter what comes my way,*
*   no matter how it comes,*
*   or when,*
YET will I rejoice in God.

I know nothing of figs and flocks
nor of diminishing herds and crop failures,
but Habakkuk's resolution
serves me well in any and all situations--
even dentist chairs and doctor's offices!

SECOND BLESSING

They all ate as much as they wanted, and they collected
what was left of the scraps, seven baskets full. Now four thousand
men had eaten. . .

Matthew15:37,38 (JB)

From Sunday School days
we know well that
five loaves plus two fishes equaled five thousand fed.
But seven loaves
plus a few small fish
equals four thousand?
Did people see this as a second class miracle,
not quite as bright or intense as the first,
same song, second verse?
Could even miracles become the same old thing--
    just another blind man,
    just one more cripple?

Have I ever received your daily mercies,
which are new every morning
as *same old, same old?*
Please, Lord, forgive me
when I take your goodness for granted.

SECOND CHANCE

(The angel said) But go, tell his disciples and Peter,
"(Jesus) is going ahead of you into Galilee. There you will see
him, just as he told you."

Mark 16:7 (NIV)

Tell his disciples--that I understand--
but Peter?
The last time I saw him
he was the one who lied,
the one who denied--
why tell him?

Because the story doesn't end there.

Yes, Peter lied
and yes, Peter denied--
but when you read on, you learn
that Peter who lied and
Peter who denied
is also Peter who cried--
    in shame,
    and remorse,
    and disbelief at his own cowardice.

Child, have you forgotten
my promise of forgiveness?
Whenever you need it,
it's yours for the asking

SENIOR CITIZEN

Listen to me. . . I have cared for you from the time you were born; I am your God and will take care of you until you are old and your hair is gray. I made you and will care for you; I will give you help and rescue you.

Isaiah 46:3,4 (GNB)

I'm there now, Lord--
    gray haired and octogenarian
and I witness that these words are true.

In my youth,
through the decades in Congo
and today in this good place
    where I live in retirement
You have walked beside me
    and gone before me
    every step of my way.

I know it will be no different
    in the days still ahead for me.
But they do say that recall is the first casualty
    as we get older,
    so, please, Lord,
jog my memory p.r.n.*

* p.r.n.= *pro re nata,* medical speak for as often as necessary.

SHEPHERDS

And in that region there were shepherds out in the field,
keeping watch over their flock by night. And an angel of the Lord
appeared to them, and the glory of the Lord shone around them. . .
                                                    Luke 2:8 (NIV)

Angels,
        a multitude of the heavenly host
        the glory of God
and shepherds
        unwashed
        unlearned--
an odd pairing, indeed.

I marvel
that the news of the birth of God's own son
was delivered not to the important
        or the religious
but to the most simple and lowly.
The only explanation I can see?
they were about the tasks for which they were responsible
and that baby grown
would equate obedience and faithfulness with love.

May I be so about the business
you have entrusted to me
that I make a climate where I can hear
both angel song
and your still small voice
directing my steps.

SIBLINGS

*Six days before the Passover festival, Jesus came to
Bethany, where Lazarus lived whom he had raised from the dead.
There a supper was given in his honor. . . Martha served and
Lazarus sat among the guests with Jesus. Mary brought a pound
of very costly perfume, pure oil of nard, and anointed the feet of
Jesus and wiped them with her hair, till the house was filled with
the fragrance.*

John 12:1-3 (NEB)

A tale of two sisters
(we know them well)
and (possibly) a tale of two hair-dos.

Martha, the older, (or so we assume)
her hair in a bun
from which no tendril of curl escaped;
she took good care of her house,
she never let the supper dishes sit till morning;
her cuisine was *cordon bleu*--
but she tended to be bossy.
Aren't big sisters meant to do that?

Mary was the little sister--
no buns or braids for her!
Luke tells us she sat at Jesus' feet
(which annoyed Martha very much)
and John adds
she anointed Jesus' feet with perfume
and used her hair to wipe them dry.
A beautiful gesture
but it could have sent Martha straight over the cliff.

We'll never know
but as a big sister myself
I think Martha may have envied Mary's freedom.
She couldn't throw out all her self-imposed directives
but she, too, loved Jesus
and they both agreed
that if Jesus had come sooner
their brother Lazarus would not have died.

Do we have to be one OR the other,
a Martha OR a Mary?
Can't people be hybrids, too?

SLEEPLESS NIGHT

*Now there was a man of the Pharisees, named Nicodemus,
a ruler of the Jews. This man came to Jesus by night. . .*
                                    John 3:1,2 (RSV)

Sometimes, Lord, that's when I've come--
in dark, still hours,
wakened by the inaudible clamor
of a problem too big for me.

I hear the clock strike three, then four,
as insistent, unanswerable questions
hammer dully on the eardrums of my spirit
or shrill in psychic decibels,
shattering my fragile equilibrium.

I need help, Lord;
may your voice of quiet authority
speak peace
to the silent roarings of my imagination
and drown out the drumming
of my fears.

STILL TO STAND

Take up God's armor... Then you will be able to stand your ground when things are at their worse, to complete every task and still to stand.

Ephesians 6:13 (NEB)

I like that, Lord--
still to stand.
Not just make it through the day
and then collapse,
but still to stand
    praising you for what you have done;
    praising you for your strength
    that has been made perfect in weakness
praising you.

Is that the secret?

STILL VALID

A verse learned in Sunday School
many years ago
apropos at the time
but what can it say to me today?

Today's *now* is very different indeed
but even though my life has become
prosaic, pedestrian and pacemaker-powered
I still rejoice in that relationship.

Yes, I have changed but
but You, God, remain ever the same.
That is what makes this verse
a word for all decades of life.

TASSELS

Everything (the Pharisees) do is done to attract attention, like wearing broader phylacteries and longer tassels.

Matthew 23:5 (JB)

Lord, show me the long tassels I tie on
so I can appear to be other than I am:
    the poses I assume,
    the phrases I pronounce,
    the roles I pretend;
they are phony, and they fool no one.

Your way is a way without guile:
    to look like what I am,
    to speak out what I think,
    to be what I am becoming in you.
The ornament of a quiet and gentle spirit
doesn't need long tassels.

THANK OFFERINGS

He who sacrifices thank offerings honors me, and he
prepares the way so that I may show him the salvation of God.
Psalm 50:23 (NIV)

Lord, I know that when I complain and fuss
I drag my spirit down
and my latter end is worse than the beginning.

I know, too, you've said I ought to praise in all things
and I recognize that when I do that
I feel better about life in general

But it never occurred to me
that my praise makes it possible
for you to intervene directly in my life.

Praise is not just an obligation--
it's a preparation
and it opens my eyes to see your light.

THREEFOLD DIRECTIVE

Be joyful always; pray continually; give thanks in all
circumstances, for this is God's will for you in Christ Jesus.
I Thessalonians 5:16-18 (NIV)

A triad of directives--
and in them I hear an echo of my mother's bedtime voice:
  Wash your face, she said;
  brush your teeth,
  and get into bed,
the whole underlined by an unspoken but unequivocal
NOW!
My sisters and I got the message.

Paul's instructions are just as easy to understand:
  Rejoice! he wrote;
  Pray!
  Give thanks!
and his interchangeable adverbs
add up to an equally emphatic NOW.

NOW--
  always,
  continually,
  in all circumstances.
I can't claim I don't understand;
help me, Lord, to put them into practice

TIME OUT

Jesus said, Make the people sit down. There was plenty of grass there. . . Then Jesus took the loaves, gave thanks, and distributed them to the people as they sat there.

John 6:10 (NEB)

Lord,
I find it hard to sit down
and just be quiet before you.
It's much easier to rush about
and be efficient--
    preparing the food
    or marshaling others into line.
My pragmatic up-and-at-it self
is restless and ill at ease
with green pastures
and still waters
but I do know
do-it-yourself
will never restore my soul.

Where would you have me sit, Lord?

TIMING

I charge you to obey your orders irreproachably and without fault until our Lord Jesus Christ appears. That appearance God will bring to pass in his own good time. . .
                                     Timothy 6:14,15 (NEB)

When I say I will do something
in my own good time,
there is in the phrase
a hint of irritation,
and you know I feel pushed
or threatened.

But, Lord, when you do something
in *your* good time,
the words mean what they say:
it is the time you have chosen of all possible times;
it is the best time in relation to all your good purposes.
With you, Lord,
there is no *too late* or *too soon:*
You know when I am ready.

TOMORROW

How often, Lord,
as I anticipate tomorrow's task
I fret and fuss about
Who? or *How?* or *When?*
and I grow cross with you
because I cannot see
the end from the beginning.
And all the while
You have already prepared
the *Who* and the *When*
as well as the *How* of it.

However big the stone, Lord,
You are bigger still--
all You ask is that I trust You.

WINESKINS

(Jesus said) Nobody puts new wine into old wine skins: if he does, the wine will burst the skins, and the wine is lost, and the skins, too. No! New wine, fresh skins.

Mark 2:22 (JB)

But, Lord,
already I am an old wineskin--
    rigid, unpliable
in so many ways.
And my church, too--
    settled in its programming,
    fixed in its ritual--
must the working of the wine of your Spirit
cause us to burst?

You who pour out the new wine,
can You not also make all things new--
    even old wineskins?

YOKEFELLOW

(Jesus said) "Bend your neck to my yoke, and learn from me, for I am gentle and humble-hearted, and your souls will find relief. For my yoke is good to bear, my load is light."
Matthew 11:28-30 (NEB)

Then something's wrong, Lord--
often I feel I have too much to bear
and the burden is so heavy
it weighs me down
and at day's end I am worn out.

Am I carrying loads not meant for me?
Or is it that I wear your yoke
but pull against it?
Either way will give me
a pain in the neck.

PERIPHERAL VISION SCRIPTURE INDEX
(Titles in text are arranged in alphabetical order.)

NEW TESTAMENT

OLD TESTAMENT

CPSIA information can be obtained at www.ICGtesting.com
Printed in the USA
LVOW082252180112

264554LV00002B/67/P

9 781600 476570